THE TABLETOP LEARNING SERIES

ARTS and CRAFTS

From Things Around the House

by Imogene Forte

Incentive Publications, Inc.
Nashville, Tennessee

Illustrated by Mary Hamilton and Gayle Seaberg Harvey
Cover designed by Mary Hamilton and illustrated by Jan Cunningham
Edited by Mary C. Mahoney and Susan Oglander

ISBN 0-86530-090-9
Library of Congress Catalog Number 83-80961

THE TABLETOP LEARNING SERIES™ is a trademark of Incentive Publications, Inc., Nashville, TN 37215

THIS
ARTS-and-CRAFTS BOOK
BELONGS TO

_____

CONTENTS

TRICKS AND TREASURES

A NOTE TO KIDS

Here are some things you need to know before you begin to use this arts-and-crafts book.

. . . First, all of the projects are fun and easy to do. You can finish any or all of them without a lot of art supplies, and you don't have to work long hours to have a finished product you can be proud of.

. . . Organize your art supplies so they are always ready for use. You will need crayons, scissors, ruler, felt tip pens, construction paper, paints, paintbrush, glue or paste, and a good pencil as basic supplies. Find a sturdy bag to hold your supplies. A paper shopping bag, last year's schoolbag, an old briefcase, and a laundry bag are some possibilities. A nylon net bag with a drawstring closure so it can be carried with you to school, in the car, to the backyard, or wherever you decide to work on your next creative project would be especially nice.

. . . Every activity tells you *what to use* and *what to do*. Always read the activity completely, from beginning to end, then gather your materials and arrange your work space before you start to work. It is also a good idea to check with the grownups to make sure that your plans meet with their approval.

. . . Try to be a neat worker and avoid clutter as you go. Cover your work area with an old sheet or tablecloth if you plan to use paints or other messy materials. This also organizes your tools and supplies and helps to keep your project all together.

. . . So select a project that interests you, grab your arts-and-crafts bag, and get set to enjoy making and doing some extraordinary things with ordinary things from around the house.

Imogene Forte

SHARING AND ENJOYING YOUR ARTS AND CRAFTS

One of the best parts of creating arts and crafts from things around the house is sharing them with others. Your friends and family members will enjoy your finished projects and will think you are very special for having made them

Here are some ways to share:
<u>pictures, collages, and other flat projects</u>
- pinned on a bulletin board
- taped to the refrigerator
- rolled up inside a tube or flat in an envelope for mailing
- glued inside a box top and covered with plastic wrap
- folded or mounted as a greeting card
- taped on someone's door or mirror as a surprise

<u>nonflat projects</u>
- in a special spot set aside as "the art spot," use different kinds of fabric or paper to show the things off. Examples: a circle, heart, or other shape cut from velvet, crepe or tissue paper, burlap, paper doilies, crumpled aluminum foil, a silk scarf, Easter grass, carpet squares, a place mat, small mirror, upturned basket or bowl, covered box

And don't forget to wrap and present some of your finished projects as gifts. Once you start using your imagination, sharing and enjoying your arts and crafts with others will be as exciting as making them.

WAIT! DON'T THROW IT AWAY!

save it for your arts-and-crafts treasure chest

- ☐ paper bags of all sizes
- ☐ used gift wrap and tissue paper
- ☐ gift cards and ribbons
- ☐ gift, tissue, candy, cereal, and other interesting boxes
- ☐ margarine, cheese, and yogurt containers
- ☐ cardboard tubes from toilet tissue, paper towels, shelf paper, or kitchen wrap
- ☐ egg cartons
- ☐ pill, perfume, and other interesting bottles
- ☐ old nylon stockings
- ☐ one-of-a-kind socks and mittens (save the one that is not worn out!)
- ☐ spools
- ☐ magazines
- ☐ nut shells
- ☐ fruit seeds and pits
- ☐ corks

- ☐ buttons, beads, and sequins
- ☐ interesting jars (jelly, mustard, olive)
- ☐ scraps of fabric of all kinds (velvet, silk, wool)
- ☐ plastic packing materials

Use a sturdy box or basket to hold your treasures and find a safe out-of-the-way place for it so it will always be handy when you are ready to work. Always make sure your materials are clean and well organized before you add them to your "treasure chest." Remember, you are collecting treasures, not junk.

SEEDS and SPICE

and other things from the kitchen

MY OWN IDEAS

KITCHEN CUPBOARD COLLAGE

be creative with your kitchen contents

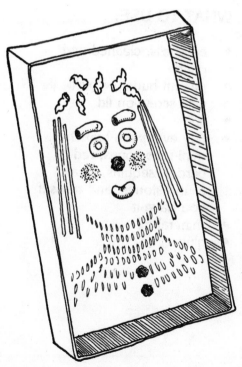

WHAT TO USE:

- dried beans
- different shapes of pasta
- rice
- dry cereal
- sunflower or other seeds
- peppercorns
- anything else you see in the cupboard that will add interest to your collage
- cardboard box top
- glue

WHAT TO DO:

1. Arrange the materials on the box top to form an interesting design. Keep moving the things around until you find a design you like. **2.** Glue your design in place.

SNOWFALL UNDER GLASS

*you can make snowflakes fall,
even on a sunny day!*

WHAT TO USE:

- eggshells, cleaned and dried
- peanut butter or pickle jar with screw-on lid
- felt
- tiny evergreen branches, mini-pine cones, red berries, sequins, small round stones, and moss if you have it
- mineral oil
- glue

WHAT TO DO:

1. Crush some eggshells into very fine pieces and set aside. **2.** Cut a piece of felt to cover the jar lid. Glue the felt into place to protect the tabletop. **3.** On the inside of the jar lid, arrange the small stones and moss into a "forest floor" for the evergreen trees. Glue into place. Decorate the tree branches with pine cones, berries, and sequins, and glue these into place on the forest floor. **4.** Let dry for ½ hour. **5.** Fill the jar with mineral oil. Add the crushed eggshells. **6.** Screw the jar lid on securely, and shake the jar gently. **7.** Turn the jar upside down and watch the snow fall on the forest.

SOAPY WAVES

for a design that won't wash away

WHAT TO USE:

- soap flakes
- blue construction paper
- pencil
- water
- mixing bowl

WHAT TO DO:

1. Draw a boat on the blue paper — a rowboat, sailboat, tugboat, ferryboat.
2. Mix the soap flakes and a little water in a mixing bowl until it forms a stiff paste.   **3.** With your fingers, carefully "paint" the soap paste on the picture to cover the boat.   **4.** When the boat is completely painted with soap paste, make some waves to show the ocean. Cover the wave lines with the soap paste too.

Variation
Make a sea animal such as a whale, dolphin, or shark instead of a boat.

KITCHEN HANG-UPS

a perfect housewarming or shower gift

WHAT TO USE:

- kitchen gadgets (cookie cutters, spoons, forks, potato peeler, tea strainer)
- wooden mixing spoon
- kitchen twine
- scissors

WHAT TO DO:

1. Gather kitchen gadgets to tie on your mobile. (They can later be cut off the mobile for use again.) **2.** Cut several equal lengths of twine to make a hanger for the mobile. Twist the lengths together to make it strong. **3.** Tie the twisted twine onto the spoon to make the hanger. **4.** Cut different lengths of twine to hold the gadgets. **5.** Tie the gadgets on to make an interesting pattern.

COOKIE MONSTERS

a monster you can gobble up

WHAT TO USE:

- large mixing bowl
- measuring cups
- wooden spoon
- measuring spoons
- waxed paper
- clean dish towel
- cookie sheet

- 1 stick butter, softened
- ½ cup powdered sugar
- ½ teaspoon lemon flavoring
- 1¼ cups flour
- ¼ teaspoon salt

WHAT TO DO:

1. Put the butter and sugar in the bowl and mix well with the wooden spoon. **2.** Stir in the lemon flavoring. **3.** Measure the flour and salt together and pour onto waxed paper. **4.** Pick up the waxed paper and shake about half the flour/salt mixture into the bowl containing the butter/sugar mixture. Use the wooden spoon to stir well. Shake the rest of the flour/salt mixture into the bowl. Stir until well mixed and smooth. **5.** Cover the bowl with the dish towel and put it in the refrigerator to chill. **6.** After an hour, take the dough out of the refrigerator. **7.** Set the oven for 375 degrees. **8.** Pinch off some dough and roll it around in your hands until it gets soft enough to shape. Mold the dough into playful monsters with fun heads, ears, legs, noses, tails, eyes, and tusks. Let your imagination run wild and see how creative you can be. **9.** Put the cookie monsters on the cookie sheet as you shape them and leave room for them to spread as they bake. **10.** Bake for about 8 to 10 minutes, until golden brown.

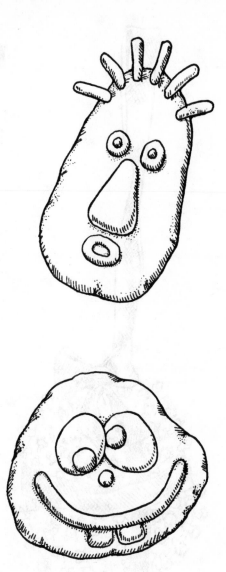

LIME AND CLOVES FOR THE NOSE!

sniff and smell — you'll think it's swell!

WHAT TO USE:

- lime or lemon
- cinnamon
- whole cloves
- ribbon
- waxed paper

WHAT TO DO:

1. Choose a large lime or lemon and wash and dry it. **2.** Cover your work surface with waxed paper. **3.** Very carefully, push the pointed ends of the cloves into the fruit until it is entirely covered with cloves. **4.** Sprinkle lots of cinnamon over the cloves. Be sure to do this over the waxed paper to catch the excess. You can roll the fruit around in the excess, but be sure not to break the cloves. **5.** Tie a pretty ribbon around the fruit and make a big bow at the top. (You may want to tie another ribbon around the fruit so it won't slip out.) **6.** Hang the fruit in the kitchen. It will give off a wonderful smell.

ART IN LIVING COLOR

a way to paint with air

WHAT TO USE:

- newspaper
- white shelf paper
- different colors of food coloring
- drinking straw

WHAT TO DO:

1. Cover your work surface with newspaper. **2.** Spread the shelf paper flat on the newspaper. **3.** Drip small blobs of food coloring all over the shelf paper. **4.** Gently blow through the straw to spread the blobs so they will mix with each other. **5.** Carefully lift the paper from side to side to mix the colors even more. **6.** Let dry on the newspaper.

FRUIT PRINTS

for fruit that leaves a lasting impression

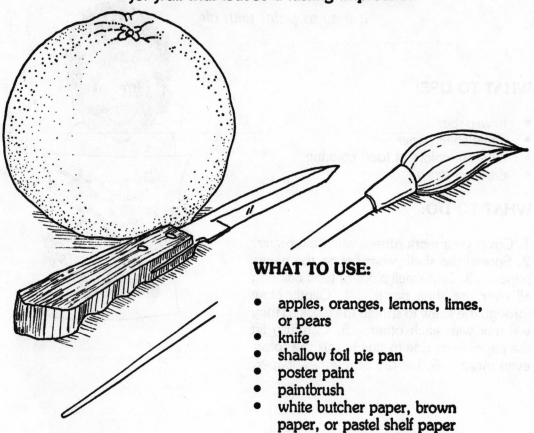

WHAT TO USE:

- apples, oranges, lemons, limes, or pears
- knife
- shallow foil pie pan
- poster paint
- paintbrush
- white butcher paper, brown paper, or pastel shelf paper

WHAT TO DO:

1. Cut a piece of fruit in half. Cut carefully to leave the seeds and texture intact. Take a minute to look at the design before you begin to work.
2. Select the color of paint you want to use, and spread it evenly in the bottom of the pie pan with the brush.
3. Press the cut side of the fruit into the paint. **4.** Press the paint-coated fruit onto the paper. Dip and press it again several times to make an attractive design to cover the paper. You will need a steady hand for this because moving the fruit will make uneven prints. **5.** Allow the paper to dry completely. You might want to use it to wrap a special present or to cover a box — or to hang on the wall.

NATURE IN THE KITCHEN

for the favorite cook in your life

WHAT TO USE:

- a full-color "nature" picture from a magazine or calendar
- cardboard
- glue
- scissors
- salt, cinnamon, toothpicks, paprika, rice, peppercorns, sesame seeds, cornmeal, brown sugar, and any other dry ingredients from the kitchen cupboard
- plastic wrap

WHAT TO DO:

1. Select a picture you really like from a magazine or calendar.   **2.** Cut it out and glue it onto the cardboard.   **3.** Look at the picture carefully and decide what areas you can cover with items from the kitchen cupboard. (Rice could be used for clouds, salt for snow, toothpicks for a fence, brown sugar for sand or paths, sesame seeds for tree trunks.)   **4.** Put glue on the picture details to be covered, working one area at a time and covering it with the desired material. Take your time and look around for more unusual things to use.   **5.** When the picture is finished, cover it tightly with plastic wrap and glue the wrap in place to preserve your nature scene.

FORK ART

scratch a few times and you'll have a design

WHAT TO USE:

- newspaper
- crayons
- white drawing paper
- old fork
- paper towel

WHAT TO DO:

1. Cover your work surface with newspaper. **2.** Use many different crayons to completely color the drawing paper. Color heavily and be sure no paper shows through. **3.** Then color over the entire surface with the black crayon. **4.** Use the prongs of the fork to scratch a pattern or design on the paper. **5.** Use the paper towel to gently brush the black crayon shavings off the drawing paper onto the newspaper to be thrown away.

YOO-HOO!
LET'S MAKE A ZANY ZOO!

make fruit and vegetables come to life

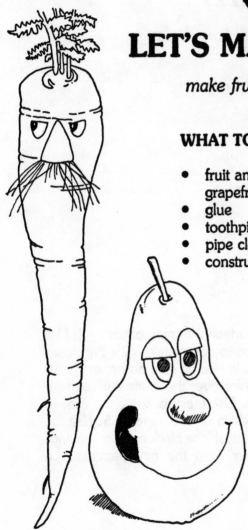

WHAT TO USE:

- fruit and vegetables (apples, potatoes, lemons, grapefruit, carrots)
- glue
- toothpicks
- pipe cleaners
- construction paper scraps

WHAT TO DO:

1. Select one fruit or vegetable you would like to turn into a zany zoo animal. **2.** Use only the materials you need to give the animal a personality all its own. **3.** If you come up with one you like the first time, you may want to keep going until you have a whole zany zoo!

30

EGGHEADS FOR THE BREAKFAST TABLE

a friend to greet you in the morning

WHAT TO USE:

- modeling clay or egg carton
- scissors
- glue
- felt tip pens
- fabric, beads, ribbon, rickrack, felt, buttons, cotton puffs, or other materials
- hard-boiled eggs

WHAT TO DO:

1. Mold a stand for each egg from modeling clay. Or cut apart an egg carton to make egg holders. **2.** Hold each egg in your hand and decide what kind of personality you want to give the egghead. **3.** Use any materials you have to make facial features, hats, collars, and jewelry. **4.** These will make great edible place cards for a special family breakfast.

31

MAKE-AND-BAKE PLAY DOUGH

create your own doughboy

WHAT TO USE:

- measuring cup
- mixing bowl
- mixing spoon
- waxed paper
- rolling pin
- cookie sheet
- knife or cookie cutters
- paintbrush
- paint
- clear shellac

- 2 cups salt
- 2 cups warm water
- 5 cups flour

WHAT TO DO:

1. Mix salt, flour, and water together. (Add water as needed to make dough easy to handle.) **2.** Knead the dough with your hands until it is smooth. **3.** Roll out with rolling pin on waxed paper to a ½-inch thickness. **4.** Use a knife or cookie cutter to cut out a shape you like and place your creation on the cookie sheet. If you want to hang your play dough creation, poke a hole at the top of it. **5.** Bake at 300 degrees for an hour. **6.** After it cools, it can be painted, then covered with clear shellac.

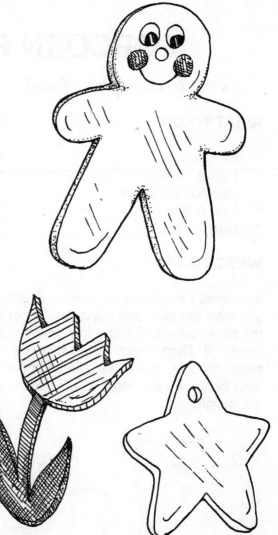

POPCORN PICTURES

some to share with a friend . . . the rest for your pictures

WHAT TO USE:

- newspaper
- manila paper or colored construction paper
- food coloring
- paper cups

- water
- popped corn
- plastic spoon
- pencil or crayon
- glue

WHAT TO DO:

1. Spread newspaper on your work surface. **2.** Decide what kind of picture you want to make, and select your paper and food coloring. **3.** Place water in the paper cups and add a few drops of food coloring to make the colors you need. **4.** Drop popcorn pieces into the cups of colored water and stir with the plastic spoon. **5.** Put the colored popcorn on the newspaper to dry. **6.** Draw your picture on the paper. **7.** Glue the colored popcorn to the paper to fill in the design.

A POT OF PASTE

for when you run dry

WHAT TO USE:

- measuring cups
- saucepan
- mixing spoon

- baby food jar or jelly jar
- construction paper
- felt tip pens
- glue
- rickrack, yarn, and other odds and ends

- 1 cup water
- ½ cup flour
- pinch of salt

WHAT TO DO:

1. Measure water and flour and mix together slowly in saucepan. **2.** Add a pinch of salt and bring to a boil over low heat. **3.** Stir until thick and glossy. **4.** While the paste is cooling, decorate the jar to hold the paste. Use scraps from the sewing box and make your own label as you like. **5.** It is a good idea to refrigerate the paste if you plan to keep it for a long period.

BEADS and BOWS

and other things from the scrap box

MY OWN IDEAS

STRING A BEAN NECKLACE

beans never looked so good

WHAT TO USE:

- lima beans in pods
- large darning needle
- heavy thread

WHAT TO DO:

1. Shell the lima beans, then separate the beans from the pods. **2.** Thread the needle with enough thread to go over your head and make your necklace the desired length. **3.** Tie a knot in one end of the thread. **4.** Push the lima beans onto the thread one at a time. Add a pod to the thread every now and then (about 1 pod for every 5 or 6 beans). **5.** Tie the ends of the thread together to finish the necklace.

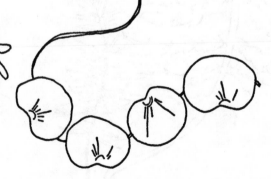

STRING A BEAN NECKLACE

WINTER WONDERLAND

make your own snow fall on the trees

WHAT TO USE:

- newspaper
- fern fronds or evergreen branches
- dark blue construction paper
- straight pins
- toothbrush
- white tempera paint or white shoe polish
- clear liquid glue
- silver glitter
- clear plastic wrap

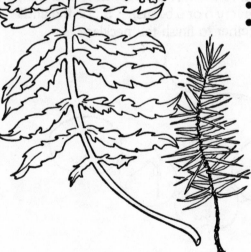

WHAT TO DO:

1. Cover a flat work space with newspaper. **2.** Lay the construction paper flat on the newspaper and arrange the fern fronds or evergreen branches on the paper to form a design you like. Pin the materials in place. **3.** Dip the toothbrush into the white paint or shoe polish. **4.** Hold the toothbrush about 6 inches from the paper and run your thumb across the bristles repeatedly in an upward direction until a nice white splattering covers the paper. **5.** Allow the paint to dry. **6.** Dab clear liquid glue on the white surfaces and sprinkle just enough silver glitter to give an icy sparkle to your picture. **7.** Remove the pins and cover the completed picture with clear plastic wrap for protection. Fold the edges of the wrap over, and glue at the corners.

MAKE A
MERRY MOBILE

these make splendid holiday decorations

WHAT TO USE:

- cardboard
- pencil
- scissors
- yarn
- wire coat hanger
- glue
- foil wrap
- assorted decorations from your scrap box

WHAT TO DO:

1. Draw lots of different shapes on the cardboard. **2.** Cut out 2 of each one. **3.** Cut different lengths of yarn. **4.** Place the 2 cardboard shapes back to back with the end of the yarn between them, and glue into place. **5.** Wrap the shape with foil. **6.** Glue on decorations to add interest. **7.** Tie the other end of the yarn around the coat hanger. **8.** Hang the merry mobile in the sunlight and watch it sparkle.

42

MINI-CUSHION

a needlework creation for someone very special

WHAT TO USE:

- 2 cloth napkins
- scissors
- darning needle
- heavy thread or yarn
- old, clean nylon stockings

WHAT TO DO:

1. Make a flower, tree, or any design using the yarn and needle on one of the cloth napkins. **2.** Sew the 2 napkins together with big stitches leaving approximately a 1½-inch margin on all sides. Be sure to leave a space large enough for you to stuff the cushion. **3.** Stuff the cushion with the stockings and sew the opening together.

43

TIE-DYED T-SHIRT

give a plain T-shirt some personality

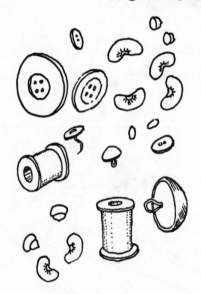

WHAT TO USE:

- 1 packet cold water dye
- cold water
- plastic dishpan
- white T-shirt
- strong thread
- dried beans and peas, empty spools, buttons
- scissors

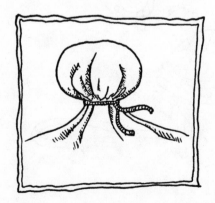

WHAT TO DO:

1. Mix the dye and cold water in the dishpan according to package directions. **2.** Place the dishpan near the cold water tap. **3.** Bunch up a piece of the T-shirt near the neck and tie it with some thread to make a "tied" space to hold the T-shirt when dipping in the dye. **4.** Tie the peas, beans, spools, and buttons into the shirt to form designs. Be sure to tie the thread very tightly underneath the materials. **5.** Put the tied shirt into the dye and leave it for about 30 minutes. **6.** Take the shirt out and rinse it well under the cold water tap. **7.** Cut all the threads with scissors to unfasten the materials. **8.** Hang the shirt up to dry and you should see an interesting design all over the shirt.

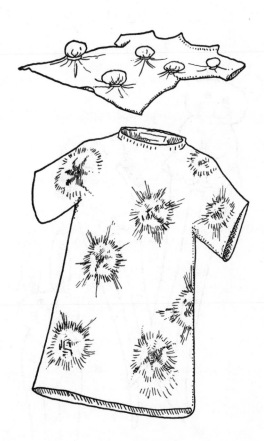

CLOTHESPIN ANIMAL PARADE

attach one to the clothesline and surprise your mom!

WHAT TO USE:

- wooden clothespins
- glue
- scissors
- fabric, felt, yarn
- felt tip pens
- paint

WHAT TO DO:

1. Decide what animals you want to make.   **2.** Use paint, felt tip pens, fabric, yarn, felt, and other items from your scrap box to decorate your clothespin animals.   **3.** Use your finished animals to set up a pet show or a circus.   **4.** You can also make up stories starring your animals and present them for your friends or younger children.

FABRIC MOSAIC

a coat of many colors

WHAT TO USE:

- fabric (the more kinds and colors the better)
- cardboard
- pencil or felt tip pen
- glue
- scissors

WHAT TO DO:

1. Cut the fabric into tiny little pieces. Try to use a lot of different colors and textures.   **2.** Draw a picture on the cardboard — a big outline of an animal or a simple scene.   **3.** Glue the fabric bits onto the picture to completely cover the drawing.

Variation
Use the fabric to make a free-form design. Glue it in place.

HANDY HANGING HOOKS

a personalized present for someone special

WHAT TO USE:

- wooden coat hangers
- metal cup hooks
- glue
- scissors
- decorations (paint, feathers, ribbon, seeds, dried weeds and flowers, nuts, material, yarn)
- paintbrush

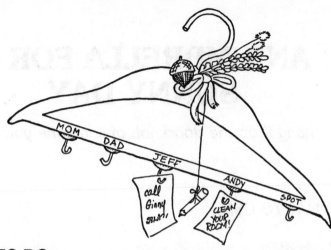

WHAT TO DO:

1. Screw the metal cup hooks at equal distances into the bottom of a wooden coat hanger. **2.** Personalize each hanger by decorating it to suit the person you are making it for.

— Paint one brown and tie on a boutonniere of grasses and seed pods. It could be used for hanging belts.

— Cover one with pretty material or yarn and tie on a bouquet of dried flowers with yarn or ribbon around the neck of the hanger. It could be used for belts, necklaces, or chains.

— Use calico to cover another one. Add a bunch of dried herbs and you have hooks for the kitchen.

— Put on as many hooks as there are people in your family. Decorate by gluing on pecans, walnuts, and acorns and tie a pen and note pad to the neck. Label each hook with a family member's name, and put it near the phone to keep up with messages and notes for each family member.

— Decorate one any way you wish and use it to hang keys.

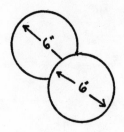

AN UMBRELLA FOR A SUNNY DAY

hang it on the doorknob of someone you like

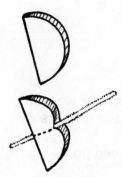

WHAT TO USE:

- scissors
- yellow and green tissue or crepe paper
- paste
- pipe cleaner
- ribbon
- lace or rickrack
- spring flowers

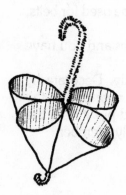

WHAT TO DO:

1. Cut a 6-inch circle from each color of paper. **2.** Paste the 2 circles together. **3.** Make a hole in the center to slip the end of a pipe cleaner through. **4.** Fold the circle in half, open it out, and fold it again so it's divided into quarters. **5.** Slip the pipe cleaner in the hole. Then bring the circle edges up to the pipe cleaner and paste them (see diagram). Be sure to put the paste on the pipe cleaner, not the paper. **6.** Bend the top of the pipe cleaner to look like a parasol handle. **7.** Tie a ribbon bow to the handle. Add lace or rickrack if you want. **8.** Fill the umbrella with tiny spring flowers. Violets, sweet peas, or pansies are lovely flowers to use, but if you don't have real flowers, artificial ones will do.

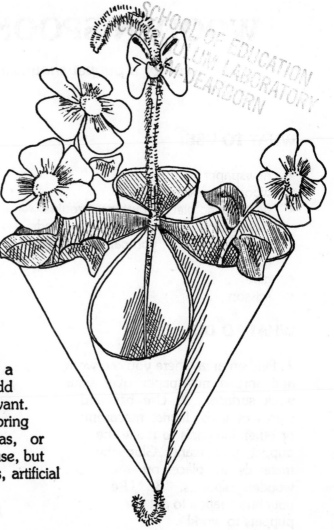

WOODEN SPOON PUPPETS

for a puppet show with friends

WHAT TO USE:

- newspaper
- wooden spoons
- yarn, fabric pieces, buttons, sequins, pipe cleaners, macaroni, cotton seeds (or whatever else you can find in a good junk box)
- glue
- scissors

WHAT TO DO:

1. Find an area where you can work and spread newspaper over your work surface. **2.** Use bits and pieces of yarn, fabric, macaroni, or other materials to make the puppet you want. Glue the materials in place on the wooden spoons. **3.** Use your imagination to put the puppets to work!

PAPER PLATE MASQUERADE

let your imagination run wild

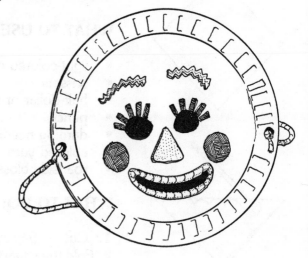

WHAT TO USE:

- paper plate
- scissors
- crayons
- yarn, rickrack, lace scraps
- glue
- elastic or strong string

WHAT TO DO:

1. Hold the paper plate up to your face and mark the places for the eyes and mouth. **2.** Cut out the eyes and mouth. **3.** Decide what kind of mask you want to make (animal, monster, king, space creature). **4.** Draw on facial features or use yarn, rickrack, lace, or other scraps to finish your mask. **5.** Carefully make small holes on either side of the mask and attach elastic or string ties.

A TISKET, A TASKET

to charm your mom and dad

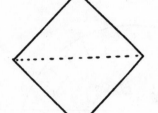

WHAT TO USE:

- light-colored construction paper
- scissors
- half-dollar or spool
- pencil
- darning needle
- colored yarn
- roadside blossoms

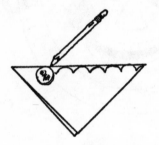

WHAT TO DO:

1. Cut a 6-inch square of construction paper. **2.** Fold the square diagonally. **3.** Use a half-dollar or spool as a pattern to scallop the folded paper. **4.** Draw several scallops in the top part of the paper, and cut out around the scallops. **5.** Thread the darning needle and sew the sides of the triangle together as shown. **6.** Make a handle from the yarn (see diagram). Attach it to the basket and tie knots at the ends to secure it. **7.** Fill the paper basket with small flowers. Roadside blossoms such as pink clover, daisies, or bluebonnets would be nice.

– A PAPER BASKET

TRICKS and TREASURES

and other things from throwaways

MY OWN IDEAS

PLAYFUL PENCIL HOLDERS

to help you keep organized

WHAT TO USE:

- empty frozen fruit juice cans or tomato paste cans
- scissors
- glue
- ribbon, rickrack, yarn, and other odds and ends
- paper baking cups
- construction paper

WHAT TO DO:

1. Wash the can and take off the label. **2.** Decide what kind of animal or character you want to create to hold your pencils. **3.** Using the various odds and ends from your scrap box, decorate a playful little friend for your desk or work space.

MAKE A SLINKY, SNEAKY SNAKE

to follow you wherever you go

WHAT TO USE:

- toilet tissue rolls or spools
- string
- construction paper, buttons, and/or yarn
- paint
- glue
- scissors

WHAT TO DO:

1. Decorate the tissue rolls to make an imaginative snake. **2.** String all the rolls together. **3.** Loop the string around the roll and tie a knot in it. **4.** Pull your snake around the yard or house.

PIE PAN WIND CHIMES

all you need is a little breeze

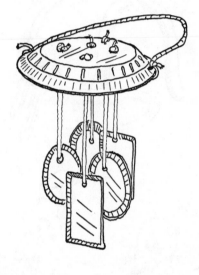

WHAT TO USE:

- 1 large foil pie or roll pan
- different-size foil pie or roll pans
- scissors
- yarn

WHAT TO DO:

1. Make a small hole near the edge of each of the pie pans except the large one. **2.** Make as many holes in the large pie pan as you have small pie pans, varying the location of the holes.   **3.** Slip a piece of yarn through each hole in the large pie pan and tie a knot at the end.   **4.** Attach the other end to a small pie pan and tie a knot. Do this until all the pie pans are attached.   **5.** Make 2 holes on either side of the large pie pan. Thread a piece of yarn through each hole, and tie a knot in each end.   **6.** Hang the wind chimes outside the door and listen to the sound.

WISH UPON A WISHBONE

and you'll have a key ring

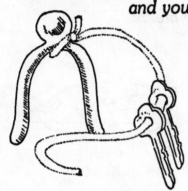

WHAT TO USE:

- dried wishbone
- poster paint
- nylon cord or yarn
- scissors
- keys
- paintbrush

WHAT TO DO:

1. Wash and dry the wishbone from your next turkey, chicken, or other fowl.
2. Leave it out to dry for about a week.
3. Paint it with your favorite color of poster paint.   **4.** Measure a piece of cord a little longer than you need to make a good-size ring to hold keys. If you use yarn instead of cord, twist or braid several strands of it together.   **5.** Tie one end of the cord tightly around the wishbone and knot it.   **6.** Slip your keys onto the other end of the cord and tie another knot to hold the keys securely on your new key ring.

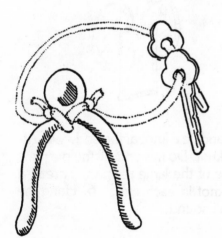

CAN A PRESENT

for a gift that's already wrapped

WHAT TO USE:

- coffee can or shortening can with a plastic lid
- scissors
- fabric
- glue
- buttons, rickrack, beads
- tissue paper
- a small-size present for a friend

WHAT TO DO:

1. Be sure the can and the lid are clean. **2.** Cut the fabric to fit around the can so that it overlaps just a little. **3.** Wrap the fabric around the can and glue it in place. **4.** Experiment with the trim until you find a design that you like. Glue the trim in place. **5.** Put some tissue paper and the present inside the can. **6.** Use some trim to decorate the lid, and put it on the can.

63

CORN SHUCK DOLL

make yourself a friend to love

WHAT TO USE:

- dried corn husks
- bowl of warm water
- string
- scissors
- buttons and beads

A TREASURE BOX FOR
TINY TRINKETS

WHAT TO DO:

1. Be sure your corn husks are completely dry. **2.** Soak them in some warm water to make them easier to handle. **3.** Fold several strong husks in half. Tie a piece of string near the fold to make a head. **4.** Beneath the tied string, insert 2 or 3 smaller husks for arms. Tie another string below the arms. **5.** Shape the bottom half of the doll into some legs or a dress. **6.** Decorate your doll with buttons and beads. If you have some fabric scraps, you can make clothes for your doll too.

65

A TREASURE BOX FOR TINY TRINKETS

a hideaway for personal secrets

WHAT TO USE:

- sturdy, small box with top
  (candy boxes and cardboard jewelry boxes work well)
- ribbon, lace, beads, sequins
- scissors
- glue

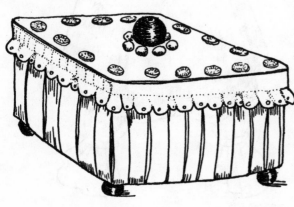

WHAT TO DO:

1. Arrange the ribbon and lace across the box and the top to create a design that completely covers the surface. **2.** Cut the ribbon and lace to fit your design. **3.** Glue the lengths of ribbon and lace in place, making sure that none of the box shows. **4.** Arrange the beads and sequins attractively on the top and glue them in place. **5.** Let dry completely.

MAKING CAT'S-EYES

a good rainy day game

WHAT TO USE:

- felt tip pens or crayons
- styrofoam meat tray
- 2 buttons
- plastic wrap or cellophane
- tape
- scissors

WHAT TO DO:

1. Draw a big cat on the bottom of the meat tray.   **2.** Color the cat with the crayons or felt tip pens.   **3.** Cut "eyes" in the cat's face slightly smaller than the 2 buttons.   **4.** Place the buttons on the tray.   **5.** Stretch the plastic wrap or cellophane tightly over the tray, wrapping it under the sides. Tape in place.

Play this game with 2 people. The object of the game is to see who can slide the buttons into place as the "cat's-eyes." Play the game with a friend or make it to give as a holiday or birthday gift to a lucky kid.

BOTTLE ART FOR YOUR TABLE

for party favors or place cards

WHAT TO USE:

- masking tape
- several small, empty bottles (the kind flavorings, food coloring, or perfume come in are good)
- paper towels
- brown liquid shoe polish
- brown yarn or ribbon
- dried flowers and twigs

WHAT TO DO:

1. Tear the masking tape into small pieces.   **2.** Completely cover the bottles with the pieces of tape. **3.** Use paper towels to rub shoe polish all over the masking tape to create an antique look.   **4.** Tie a bow around the bottle.   **5.** Put some interesting weeds, twigs, or flowers in the bottles.

ROLY-POLY CRITTERS

a chance to create a friend

WHAT TO USE:

- cardboard rolls from paper towels
- tissue or construction paper
- scissors
- glue
- yarn, buttons, other things from your "art bag"

WHAT TO DO:

1. Stand the roll up and decide what kind of roly-poly critter you want to make.   **2.** Cut the tissue or construction paper to completely cover the roll, leaving enough paper to turn in at either end. **3.** Cut and/or glue on legs, feet, hands, faces, hair, hats, clothes, or whatever you like to give your roly-poly critter a personality all its own.

THE NAME'S THE GAME

an art game for the whole family

WHAT TO USE:

- newspapers, junk mail, old magazines, empty cereal boxes
- paper place mats
- scissors
- glue
- felt tip pens

WHAT TO DO:

1. Each person is to look through newspapers, junk mail, magazines, and empty cereal boxes to find letters to spell his or her own name in as many clever and creative ways as possible, using different styles of letters, colors, and shapes. **2.** The letters are then cut out and glued onto the place mats. Try to cover the entire place mat. **3.** Other features can be added with felt tip pens to personalize your place mat even more.

The object of this activity can be to see who can get his or her name glued down the most times in a specified amount of time. No letters of names can be written; all must be found and glued.

Variation
Cut out shapes related to a specific holiday such as Halloween, Christmas, or Valentine's Day.

MILK CARTON PUPPET MOPPET

surprise someone with a puppet play

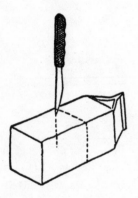

WHAT TO USE:

- 1-quart milk carton, rinsed out and dried
- knife
- construction paper, buttons, fabric, and other materials

WHAT TO DO:

1. Use a knife to slit the carton in half, cutting through only 3 sides (see diagram).   **2.** Fold it back so your hand fits inside.   **3.** Use construction paper, buttons, fabric, or other materials from your "art bag" to make eyes, ears, nose, hair, tongue, or other creative features for your puppet moppet.   **4.** Put your hand inside, and make your puppet come alive.

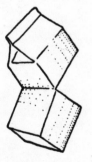

72

MONEY IN THE BANK

a place to put your pennies

WHAT TO USE:

- empty oatmeal box with top
- coins
- tissue paper
- soft lead pencil
- glue
- scissors

WHAT TO DO:

1. Glue the top on the oatmeal box. **2.** Place the coins under the tissue paper on a smooth surface. **3.** Use the pencil to go back and forth over the coins until the outlines of the coins appear. (Be careful not to get pencil marks on the other part of the tissue paper.) **4.** Completely cover the box (including the top) with the coin-dotted tissue paper. Glue it in place. **5.** Use the scissors to cut a slit in the top of the box large enough to push coins through, and begin saving for something you want to buy for yourself or someone else.

MAKE YOUR OWN THING-A-MA-JIG

and leave your friends guessing what it is

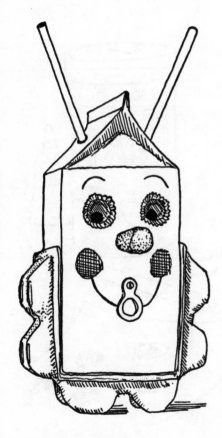

WHAT TO USE:

- newspaper
- any of these things — egg or different-size milk cartons, cheese and butter tubs, or other objects from your treasure chest
- scissors
- glue
- masking tape (if you have it)
- paint and/or felt tip pens

WHAT TO DO:

1. Clean and save empty containers until you have an interesting collection. **2.** Find a nice, big flat area to work in and cover the space with newspaper. **3.** Begin arranging the containers on top, beside, and around each other until an idea comes to you for your thing-a-ma-jig. Use your imagination and try to construct a truly creative product. It may be a building, spaceship, animal, or whatever you want. **4.** Glue or tape it all together. **5.** Use paint and felt tip pens to add the finishing touches.

74

PAPER DOLL MAGIC

a fast way to make some new friends

WHAT TO USE:

- newspaper
- scissors
- pencil
- construction paper
- glue
- ribbon, feathers, buttons, fabric pieces, and other materials
- crayons, felt tip pens

WHAT TO DO:

1. Fold a piece of newspaper accordion-style into sections of equal size.
2. On the top piece, draw a doll. Be sure that it touches each of the edges of the paper at some point.   **3.** Cut out the doll along the lines, but don't cut through any folds. You should then have a line of dolls that are attached to each other.   **4.** Use your imagination and your materials to decorate the paper dolls as you wish.

SHAPES TO FEEL

use it with a friend or make it as a gift for a younger child

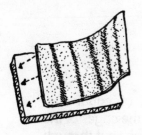

WHAT TO USE:

- shoe box
- cardboard
- old sock
- glue
- scissors
- scraps of velvet, sandpaper, sponge, satin, plastic, corduroy

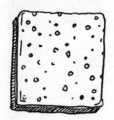

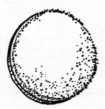

76

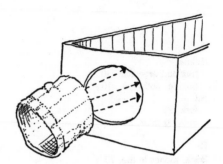

WHAT TO DO:

1. Cut 2 squares, triangles, circles, rectangles, hearts and crescents out of cardboard. **2.** Cut matching material scraps for each shape and glue on the cardboard. **3.** Glue one set of shapes to the top of the shoe box. **4.** Cut a hole in one end of the shoe box large enough for your hand. **5.** Cut the top off an old sock and glue that to the hole in the end of the shoe box. **6.** Place the other set of shapes inside the box, and glue the top onto the shoe box. **7.** Put your hand through the sock top and feel one of the shapes of material. Say aloud which one you think you have chosen, then remove it and place it on the matching shape on the top of the box. Continue until you have matched all the shapes correctly.

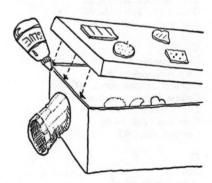

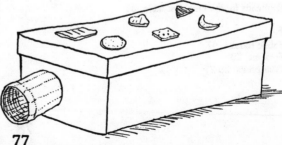

INDEX